A-6 INTRUDER
IN ACTION

by LOU DRENDEL

squadron/signal publications

Photo Credits:
USAF
US Navy
US Marine Corps
Norman E Taylor
CDR Don Boecker
Dr J G Handleman
Bruce Trombecky
Bob LaBouy
H Nagakubo
S Ohtaki
Roger Besecker
Lou Drendel
Jim Sullivan
Peter Mancus
Grumman
Jim Brady
Bruce Smith
Duane Kasulka
Jan Jacobs
Charles Howes

Introduction...

It has often been said that necessity is the mother of invention. It has also been said that what the mind of man can conceive, the mind of man can accomplish. The Korean War very graphically demonstrated the necessity of an all-weather attack airplane, but conception of the A-6 concept did not occur (formally) until 1956, at which time the U.S. Navy formulated requirements for a day/night all-weather attack aircraft, capable of delivering conventional or nuclear weapons. The Admirals hadn't been sitting on their hands all through the early fifties . . . they just realized that existing state-of-the-art technology wouldn't allow the development of what they really needed. But by 1956 technological horizons were expanding rapidly, and the word went out to the aircraft manufacturers.

Seven manufacturers submitted eleven different proposals and on New Year's Eve, 1957, Grumman design 128 emerged victorious. It was immediately christened the A2F-1 by the Navy. The development contract was signed the following May, and in April of 59' a production contract was awarded. The first A-6A made it's first flight one year later. Testing and trials lasted for nearly three years, the first A-6's being delivered to the fleet in February, 1963 as the Atlantic Fleet Replacement Squadron (VA-42) took delivery of the first two of it's Intruders. One year later VA-75 "Sunday Punchers" became the first operational Intruder Squadron, joining Air Wing Seven, aboard the USS Independence.

If the design of it's airframe is less than breathtakingly beautiful, the A-6's avionics more than make up for the lack of visual aesthetics. The Intruder is simply an all-weather wonder. It is the first aircraft to breach those far technological horizons hinted at during the fifties. And the basically sound airframe has hosted hundreds of changes over the years, as space-age technology came of age by leaps and bounds.

DIANE (Digital Integrated Attack and Navigation Equipment) is at the heart of the A-6's remarkable capability. It allows the Intruder crew to take off, fly to pre-selected targets at any altitude, deliver ordnance, and return to base without ever looking outside of the cockpit . . . all without the aid of any but the Intruder self-contained navigation aids! They can also change targets in mid-mission, without losing any of their capability.

The number three A-6 (BuNo 147866) at MCAS Cherry Point, N.C. in 1962. At that time it was designated A2F-1Q. (USMC)

The number five A-6 in slow flight during fuel dumping tests. Smaller vertical fin and lack of refueling probe readily identifies prototype A-6's. (above) Later test model of the Intruder undergoing Carrier Suitability Tests at the hands of NATC test pilots. It is about to be launched with the max ordnance load of 15,000 lbs. (left) The number 26 aircraft undergoing further NATC tests. Larger vertical fin, with ECM antenna, has been added, though pitot tube is still carried on port wing rather than above tail anti-collision light as in later models. (below) (all U.S. Navy)

A-6A of NATC's Weapons System Test Division during a visit to NAS Glenview in 1969. Nose gear door contains anti-collision and taxi lights, as well as an ECM antenna. (Lou Drendel)

Prototype EA-6A about to "trap" during carrier suitability tests. EA-6's do not have wingtip speed brakes, relying exclusively upon the fuselage speed brakes for aerodynamic braking. (Grumman)

Preparing an A-6A of the Naval Missile Center for a flight from the Center's Point Mugu, Calif. facility. It is carrying a "buddypack" refueling pod on the centerline. (Peter Mancus via Jim Sullivan)

Ejection Seat

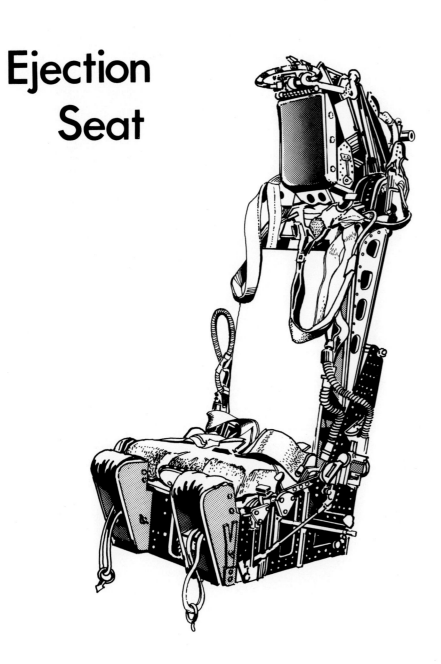

Tail Development

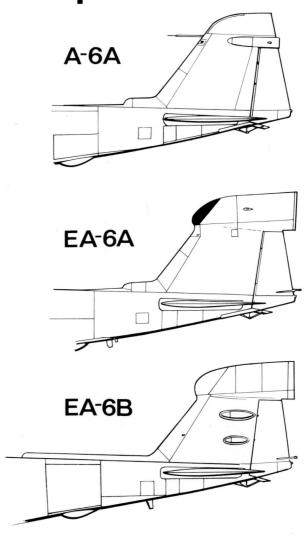

A-6A

EA-6A

EA-6B

PILOT'S PANELS

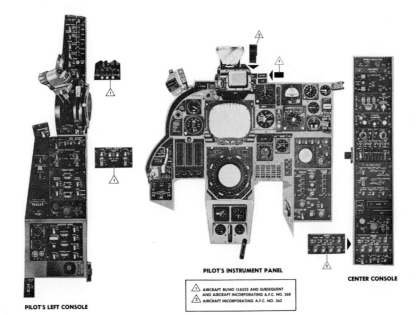

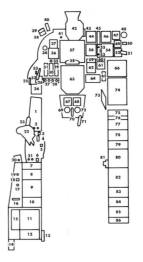

PILOT'S INSTRUMENT PANEL

CENTER CONSOLE

△1 AIRCRAFT BUNO 158533 AND SUBSEQUENT AND AIRCRAFT INCORPORATING A.F.C. NO. 268
△2 AIRCRAFT INCORPORATING A.F.C. NO. 263

PILOT'S LEFT CONSOLE

PILOT'S LEFT CONSOLE
1. FUEL MANAGEMENT CONTROL PANEL
2. SPEED DRIVE SWITCH
3. SPIN RECOVERY SWITCH
4. FLAP LEVER
5. THROTTLE FRICTION LEVER
6. EMERGENCY FLAP SWITCH
7. APC/ANTI-SKID/FLAPERON POP-UP PANEL
8. GENERATOR/ENGINE AND FUEL PANEL
9. SIGHT UNIT CONTROL PANEL
10. PILOT'S ICS PANEL
11. MASTER LIGHT CONTROL PANEL
12. G-VALVE TEST BUTTON
13. RAM AIR TURBINE HANDLE
14. BACK-UP HYDRAULIC SYSTEM TEST SWITCH
15. AUXILIARY UHF RECEIVER PANEL ARP 45 ARP 50
16. VENT SUIT-SEAT CUSHION CONTROL
17. OXYGEN SWITCH
18. RUDDER TRIM SWITCH
19. ARRESTING HOOK POSITION WARNING BY-PASS SWITCH
20. SPEED BRAKE TEST SWITCH
21. CRANK SWITCHES
22. THROTTLES
23. CATAPULT GRIP

PILOT'S INSTRUMENT PANEL
24. INTEGRATED POSITION INDICATOR
25. BRAKE SELECTOR HANDLE
26. HYDRAULIC PRESSURE INDICATORS
27. POWER TRIM INDICATORS
28. OIL PRESSURE INDICATORS
29. FUEL FLOW INDICATOR
30. EXHAUST GAS TEMPERATURE INDICATOR
31. ENGINE RPM INDICATOR
32. LANDING GEAR HANDLE
33. LANDING GEAR OVERRIDE HANDLE
34. EMERGENCY STORES JETTISON BUTTON
35. LOW ALTITUDE WARNING LAMP
36. RADAR ALTIMETER
37. ANGLE OF ATTACK INDICATOR
38. APCS STANDBY LIGHT
39. WHEELS WARNING LIGHT
40. APPROACH INDEXER

41. MASTER CAUTION RESET BUTTON
42. OPTICAL SIGHT
43. DECM CONTROL PANEL
44. MACH/AIR SPEED INDICATOR
45. "G" METER
46. VERTICAL GYRO INDICATOR
47. CLOCK
48. OXYGEN QUANTITY GAGE
49. RATE OF CLIMB INDICATOR
50. CANOPY SWITCH
51. CANOPY EMERGENCY JETTISON HANDLE
52. MD-1 TURN AND SLIP INDICATOR
53. HOOK LIFT BUTTON
54. HORIZONTAL SITUATION INDICATOR
55. GYRO FAST ERECT BUTTON
56. SERVOED BAROMETRIC ALTIMETER
57. VERTICAL DISPLAY INDICATOR
58. SLIP/SKID INDICATOR
59. UHF CHANNEL/FREQUENCY
60. HOOK RELEASE HANDLE
61. 8-6 ACCELEROMETER
62. FUEL QUANTITY GAGE
63. PILOT'S HORIZONTAL DISPLAY
64. ANNUNCIATOR PANEL
65. MASTER TEST PANEL
66. ECM WARNING CONTROL PANEL
67. AUXILIARY BRAKE CYCLE GAGE
68. CABIN PRESSURE ALTITUDE GAGE
69. STABILIZER TRIM GAGE
70. RUDDER PEDAL ADJUST CONTROL
71. MANUAL CANOPY HANDLE
72. RUDDER TRIM GAGE
73. FOOT HEAT CONTROL
74. PILOT'S CONTROL PANEL

CENTER CONSOLE
75. THREAT INDICATOR
76. GCBS ADDRESS PANEL
77. AUTOPILOT CONTROL PANEL
78. UHF COMMUNICATIONS PANEL
79. ZACAN PANEL
80. TRANSPONDER-IFF/APX CONTROL
81. AUX. HYD. PUMP BUTTON
82. AIR CONDITIONING CONTROL PANEL
83. WING FOLD CONTROL PANEL
84. B/N's ICS CONTROL PANEL
85. PILOT'S RADIO CONTROL PANEL
86. ANT SEL/CABIN DUMP/CNI MASTER CONTROL PANEL

A-ADF1-50

BOMBARDIER/ NAVIGATOR'S PANELS

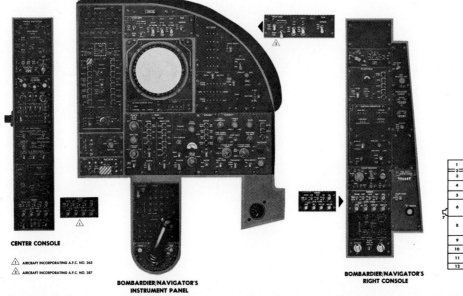

AFT BULKHEAD CONSOLE

CENTER CONSOLE

△1 AIRCRAFT INCORPORATING A.F.C. NO. 263
△2 AIRCRAFT INCORPORATING A.F.C. NO. 287

BOMBARDIER/NAVIGATOR'S INSTRUMENT PANEL

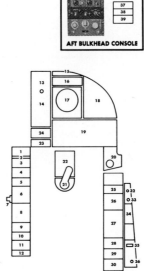

BOMBARDIER/NAVIGATOR'S RIGHT CONSOLE

CENTER CONSOLE
1. THREAT INDICATOR
2. GCBS ADDRESS PANEL
3. AUTOPILOT CONTROL PANEL
4. UHF COMMUNICATIONS PANEL
5. TACAN PANEL
6. TRANSPONDER-IFF/APX CONTROL
7. AUX. HYD. PUMP BUTTON
8. AIR CONDITIONING CONTROL PANEL
9. WING FOLD CONTROL PANEL
10. B/N's ICS CONTROL PANEL
11. PILOT'S RADIO CONTROL PANEL
12. ANT SEL/CABIN DUMP/CNI MASTER CONTROL PANEL

BOMBARDIER/NAVIGATOR'S INSTRUMENT PANEL
13. MASTER ARMAMENT SWITCH
14. ARMAMENT CONTROL UNIT
15. MASTER CAUTION PANEL
16. ECM CONTROL PANEL
17. DIRECT VIEW RADAR INDICATOR
18. DIGITAL DISPLAY UNIT
19. BOMBARDIER NAVIGATOR'S CONTROL PANEL
20. OUTSIDE AIR TEMPERATURE GAGE
21. SLEW CONTROL
22. COMPUTER CONTROL UNIT (KEYBOARD)
23. NUCLEAR CONTROL PANEL
24. AWW-4 FUZING PANEL

BOMBARDIER/NAVIGATOR'S RIGHT CONSOLE
25. DOPPLER CONTROL PANEL
26. PLATFORM CONTROL PANEL
27. ERECTION CONTROLLER
28. VIDEO TAPE RECORDER
29. RADIO CONTROL PANEL
30. CHAFF DISPENSER CONTROL PANEL
31. GROUND CONTROL BOMBING SYSTEM CONTROL PANEL
32. OXYGEN LEVER
33. MASTER TEST BUTTON
34. INTERIOR LIGHTING CONTROL PANEL
35. VENT SUIT-SEAT CUSHION CONTROL
36. G-VALVE TEST BUTTON

AFT BULKHEAD CONSOLE
37. RADAR BEACON CONTROL PANEL
38. KY-28 CONTROL PANEL
39. MA-1 COMPASS CONTROL PANEL

7

A-6 INTRUDER

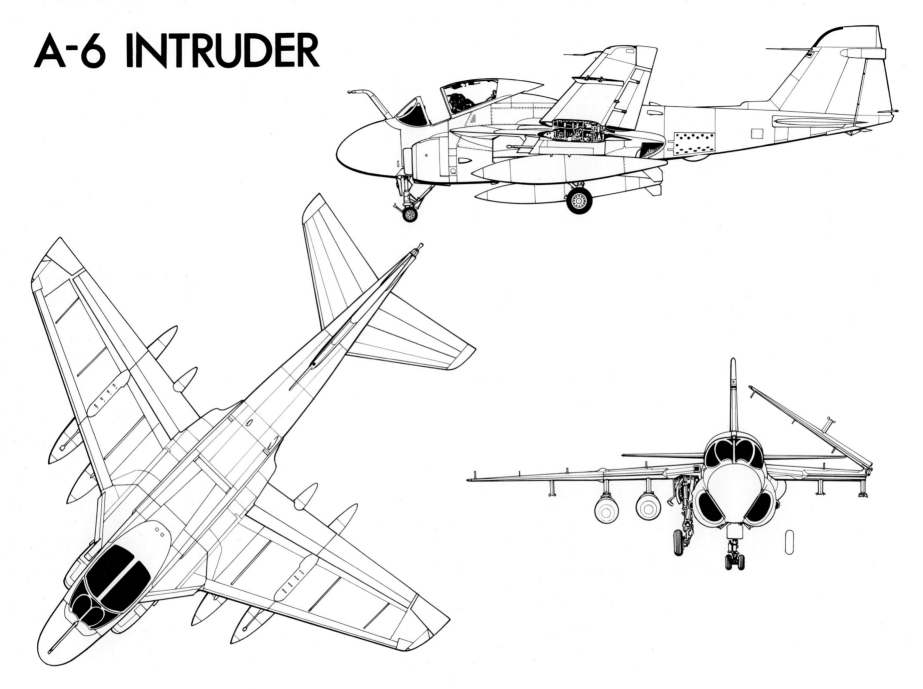

KA-6 Details

9

To War

Commander Donald V. Boecker is currently the Commanding Officer of VA-85. As a member of VA-75 in the early sixties, he was one of the pilots who introduced the A-6 to fleet service, and took it into combat for the first time. This is his story of those experiences.

"I checked into VA-75 in 1963. At the time VA-75 was still an A-1 squadron, and was scheduled to become the first A-6 squadron. There were about 110 people assigned, and the squadron still had three A-1's which had not yet been transferred to other A-1 squadrons. I was assigned the job of personnel officer, which meant that I had to check in all new people, and check out all of the A-1 personnel who were going to other fleet A-1 squadrons. This was quite an undertaking, since we retained very few of the original VA-75 complement. In addition to transferring the A-1 personnel, I had to check in the 330 new A-6 personnel who had been drawn from various jet attack squadrons throughout the fleet. Since we were the first A-6 squadron, and the A-6 was the first really all-weather attack aircraft the Navy had, the squadron received some of the best people in the Navy.

The first order of business was a maintenance school, followed by an examination. We then began our flying with VA-42, the A-6 Replacement Squadron. We were all thoroughly impressed with the A-6, and enjoyed the flying immensely.

The Squadron finished the RAG in February, 1964, and was assigned to Air Wing Seven, (CVW-7) aboard the USS INDEPENDENCE (CVA-62). At that time the Independence was still in the Mediterranean, completing a seven month cruise. Consequently, we did our qualifications (CARQUALS) aboard two other ships. Our day CarQuals were accomplished aboard the USS Saratoga (CVA-60) and night CarQuals were completed on the USS Forrestal (CVA-59).

After our CarQuals, we began an intensive program of full-system bombing at Tangier Target. Tangier Target is an old freighter, which is partially sunk in the Chesapeake Bay, off Tangier Island, which is 80 miles north of Norfolk. The Mayor of Tangier Island calls the target spots to the aircrews who do their bombing there. One of the memorable events of that period was the dropping of the 100,000th bomb on Tangier Target. Pete Easton, one of our pilots, did the job, and was rewarded with a helicopter trip to the island, and a ceremony put on by the Mayor, complete with a cake to mark the occasion.

In the fall of 1964, we moved aboard the USS Independence for a two week cruise up to the World's Fair at New York City. We were to showcase the USS Independence, her airwing, and our brand new A-6 Squadron. During our stay there the officers of VA-75 were feted at a cocktail party atop the Time-Life Building, which was sponsored by Grumman. Grumman also arranged tours of the city for us, and a three-day golf weekend. After eight days in New York, we sailed,

VA-42 Intruders during training flight in 1963. (above) (USN) Don Boecker and A-6A aboard USS Independence, circa 1965. Note interesting variation of Tonkin Gulf Yacht Club patch. (Don Boecker) (below)

spending five days in the return to Norfolk. During this time we conducted air operations and sharpened our skills.

For the four months following this short cruise, we operated out of NAS Oceana, conducting training flights to Tangier Target, and various low-level missions into the mountains of North Carolina, Virginia, and Tennessee. During this time VA-75 became a real family. We had a

A-6A of LCDR Deke Bordone. Tail numbers and letters are black, edged with red. (U.S. Navy)

weekly happy hour gathering every Friday, and twice a month the wives would join in for dinner and dancing afterwards.

Early in 1965 we moved aboard USS Independence for a short cruise to the Carribbean. We were notified that we would be departing for Westpac in May. During this cruise we intensified our training, practicing weapon delivery on the island of Viecas, which is between St. Thomas and Puerto Rico. The bombing of North Vietnam had begun in earnest, and we anticipated going to war, so the training took on additional meaning.

Upon our return to Norfolk, preparations got underway for our Westpac cruise. We were given daily briefings on some aspect of the cruise, either on the latest intelligence, or on some personal aspect of going to war. We got twelve brand new airplanes, right off the assembly lines with all the latest modifications installed.

We left about May 1, and I'll never forget that day. It was one of the real sad experiences of my life. All of the crew's families lining the pier to wave, some of them seeing each other for the last time. One of the sad personal incidents of that leave-taking was related to me, by my wife Bobi, when we returned. She was standing on the pier with the wife of our Executive Officer, Commander Mike Vogt. As we pulled out, Commander Vogt's wife turned to Bobi and said that she had the feeling that she would never see her husband again. Her feeling proved all too accurate, as Commander Vogt was later killed on a mission over North Vietnam.

We steamed down to Puerto Rico, where we held an ORI (Operational Readiness Inspection), simulating an actual at-sea war period. Upon completion of the ORI we spent two days and nights at St. Thomas, giving everyone a chance at liberty before the long voyage around the tip of Africa and through the Indian Ocean.

Our next stop was Singapore. During our stay there, the officers of VA-75 had an ADMIN ashore at the Regal Hotel, which was an elegant holdover from the days of British colonialism. Eight of us in the Squadron were avid golfers and by working through the U.S. Embassy, we obtained permission to play the Royal Singapore Island Country Club, which was later featured on Shell's Wonderful World of Golf. We had four Malaysian caddies, probably about fifteen years old. I'll never forget the first hole on that round. We walked to the first tee, and the yardage marker said 370 yards. There was a big valley between the tee and green though, and it looked more like 280 to me. I took out my driver and hit one of the best shots I had ever hit. The ball hit short and rolled right up on the green! I then proceeded to sink a 30 foot putt for an eagle. Well, from that point on I was king to those caddies . . . they had never seen that done before. I didn't shoot that well for the rest of the round . . . 82 I think . . . but that first hole made my day.

We left Singapore and steamed up to Cubi Point in the Phillipines, where we began our last tune-up before going into combat. It had been about a month since we had last flown, so we were a little rusty and were grateful for the chance to fly between Singapore and Cubi, and to

11

drop practice bombs on the SPAR, which is the target that is towed behind the carrier. We got our last-minute briefings and, prior to leaving Cubi, all crewmembers who were going to fly over North Vietnam were required to go through a one day survival school. The instructors for this course were former Fillipino guerillas, and they schooled us in the art of finding food in the jungle and evading the enemy. This one day school supplemented the one week course we had all gone through in the States.

Finally we reboarded the USS Independence and headed for Vietnam. Enroute we were thoroughly briefed concerning the do's and don'ts of flying over Vietnam.

The next day we flew our first combat missions. We were on what came to be known as "Dixie Station", and we flew into South Vietnam. An Air Force FAC, flying an 0-1, called us in on an enemy bunker complex. He fired his smoke rockets, then instructed us to bomb 50 meters to the north. We rolled in and dropped on his target, which we never really saw. There was no anti-aircraft fire. After we pulled off target, he gave us a bomb damage assessment, and credited us with destroying the bunkers. We headed back to the ship. I don't know what I had expected, but this was certainly anti-climactic. I thought; "If this is what combat is like, it's sure not going to be very exciting!" I didn't know how wrong I was, but I didn't have long to wait to find out.

We spent about three or four days on "Dixie Station", then moved north to begin the war in earnest. It was about the first of July, 1965.

I remember vividly the fourth of July mission that I flew. I had five Mk 84 2,000 pound bombs on my aircraft, and they were really decorated for the occasion! It didn't take the ordnancemen long to pick up on the time-honored custom of decorating our bombs with uncomplimentary salutations to the enemy. I think the favorite was, "Ho Chi Minh is a Son of a Bitch!" . . . It became so popular that it was usually abbreviated to HCMIASOB . . . after all, we never expected them to be able to read it anyway. But the bomb loaders often added to it. One I remember is, "Mary and Jane from Norfolk send their greetings to you . . . HCMIASOB!"

On July 14th we were number two in a flight of two A-6A's assigned to crater a road near Sam Nua in northern Laos. My flight lead was LCDR Bill Ruby. My Bombadier/Navigator was Don Eaton. We were carrying five Mk-82 500 lb. bombs, one on each station, because of a shortage of bombs. The target was several hundred miles from the ship. Shortly after take-off and rendezvous, LCDR Ruby's aircraft system went "down" and he passed the lead to us. We led the flight to the target at 25,000 feet, and arrived in the target area about 6 o'clock in the afternoon.

We armed our bombs and rolled in on the target. The bombs were set to become armed four and a half seconds after leaving the airplane and to detonate upon impact with the ground. The target elevation was 3500 feet above sea level. We rolled in at 18,000 feet and at 9,000 I had a good target picture, so I "pickled" as briefed at 5500 feet AGL. There was an immediate heavy explosion under the starboard wing. The port wing

Don Boecker (left) and Don Eaton. (CDR Don Boecker)

dropped about ten to fifteen degrees, and the starboard fire warning light came on. I told Don that I was securing the right engine and pulled the throttle back while pulling out of the dive. I went to 100% on the port engine and began to slowly climb out while we made a damage assessment. Within seconds we lost 2,000 pounds of wing fuel, and there was a rapid pitch-up of the right wing, so we assumed that one of the bombs had gone off either on the rack, or immediately after release. We looked back at the wings and couldn't spot any holes in either of them, but the fuel was streaming heavily from the trailing edges of both wings. We were doing rapid mental calculations, trying to figure how much fuel we had, how fast we were losing it, how long it would last with the one engine going at 100%, where the nearest divert field was, where the nearest tanker was . . . when suddenly it all became academic. The port engine fire warning light came on! This was followed by a rapid loss of hydraulic pressure. The control stick locked in a ten degree nose-down, port wing low position. I told Don that we were going to have to get out. That was seconded by LCDR Ruby, who transmitted, "You're on fire! **EJECT!**" I went to slap Don on the leg to tell him to eject, but he was practically gone by then. I waited a couple of microseconds, then pulled the face curtain myself.

Since we were below the altitude that the barostat initiates the automatic sequence when we ejected, there was no delay at all in the beginning of that sequence, and before I knew what was happening I was hanging in my chute.

I looked around and saw our airplane, in a gentle turn, diving toward the ground. I also saw Don and, even though he had ejected before me, I was passing him up due to the difference in our weight. (I'm a 200 pounder, while he weighed about 140.) I looked back at our airplane, just in time to see it fly into the side of a mountain. There was the initial impact, then a tremendous secondary explosion that appeared to totally demolish the wreckage.

The ground was getting closer and, much to my consternation, I saw that I was heading right for a small village. I could see people in the village pointing at me, and I thought they were going to shoot at me as I descended. I sure didn't want to land anywhere near any people, for obvious reasons, and I began to frantically pull on the risers, trying to steer clear of the village. I didn't seem to be able to influence my glide path though and just when it looked as though I was going to hit right in the middle of the village, a fortuitous gust of wind caught me and drifted me over a little hill and I landed about 200 yards to the southeast. Just before I landed, I could see armed soldiers running out of the village in my direction.

The area I landed in was marshy, with bull rushes about ten feet high. My chute caught in a 20 foot tree, but I made a soft landing in the weeds. I immediately released my rocket-jet fittings, took off my helmet, and prepared to get out of there.

In the meantime, Don Eaton was not fairing so well. In the early model A-6's, the procedure was to eject through the canopy. The top of the seat contained a canopy breaker that was supposed to shatter the canopy. This, combined with the greater cockpit pressurization, which caused the plexiglas to explode outward, would make a hole for the crewman to get through. Apparently something didn't work quite right, because his hands were severely bruised on the way out of the airplane. His opening shock was heavy too, with his pistol, which he had strapped down in front of him, banging him hard in the stomach. To make his misery more complete, he landed in tall grass, which caused him to misjudge his altitude, and he hurt his back with a hard landing on hard ground.

I had to make some quick decisions on what to take, and in which direction to run. I looked around and saw that Don was going to land on the other side of a large, grassy hill to my south. That direction was out . . . I'd never get over that hill before the enemy caught up to, and shot me. To the north there was another hill, but unlike the grass covered hill to the south, this one was a tangle of thick jungle undergrowth. That looked like the best bet for cover and concealment. I grabbed my survival equipment out of the parachute seat pan, and in the process accidentally actuated the nitrogen bottle that blows up the one man life raft. Frantically, I picked up the raft, and, with the superhuman strength born of fear and adrenalin, ripped it apart and threw it aside. Several times, in subsequent years, I have tried to duplicate this feat without success. Finally, with my survival equipment in hand, I took off for the hill. I crossed a little stream and plunged into a rice paddy. I didn't get ten feet into the paddy before I realized that I would never get to the other side fast enough . . . the mud was just too thick. I doubled back to the dike and took off around the paddy. I crossed a heavily traveled foot path and was into the jungle. I started up the hill, my mind spitting out the things I had learned in survival school like a computer. I was careful not to unnecessarily break any branches and I tried to leave the bush as it had been before I came through. After about a hundred feet of this, I came to what looked like an ideal hiding place, an animal den, and I burrowed into the hole, pulling underbrush over me. I barely had time to catch my breath before I heard about ten or fifteen men beating the brush, and hollering back and forth to each other in their native tongue. They had found my chute and were actively searching for me! We had ejected about 1830 local time, and I knew that the sun went down about 1930. It was now about 1900 . . . I figured that if they didn't find me before dark, I would be able to put some more distance between us during the night. I stayed put, really sweating it out . . . thinking that it would never get dark. It finally did though, but the voices persisted in their search until 2200, when they finally faded off into the distance.

I stayed hidden for another two hours, then decided to move to a spot farther away from the village. I took off my torso harness and G suit, removed my compass, knife, and other survival equipment, buried the harness and G suit in the animal den, and started to move away. About that time, I heard some strange, almost mechanical noises. The sounds were coming from the valley below me and they almost sounded like crickets to me. Don also heard them from his position, and he described them as sounding like squeaky fan belts, or possibly a truck with bad valves. We never figured out what they were, and they only lasted about a half an hour, but they appeared to have been some sort of signals from man to man.

I started off to the northwest, aiming for the top of the hill. It took me the better part of three hours to make it. The undergrowth was extremely thick, and I had to move on my hands and knees part of the time, and even on my stomach at other times. I wanted to get to the thickest part of the jungle, and that's where I ended up! The trees at the top of the hill were too high to allow a helicopter rescue, and I felt sure that the helicopters would be there at first light, so I made my way back down the hill about 20 or 30 yards to a point where the underbrush was quite thick, but at the same time, the trees were not so high. I stayed there the rest of the night, unable to sleep . . . I was still pretty well pumped up, and it was extremely cold because of the high elevation.

About 0500 the next morning, I heard an aircraft overhead. It was still dark, and the airplane was way up high, so I though it was probably a commercial aircraft. But when the sun came up at 0630, I looked up and there was a C-54 circling overhead. The night before I had checked out my survival radio, making sure that the battery was connected and that it worked properly. The homing beeper was so noisy though that I was afraid to use it, so when I spotted the C-54 I called them. No answer. I called repeatedly while it circled, but still no answer.

Boecker and Eaton eject from their stricken Intruder.

About 0715, four A-1's showed up. I called them, but got no answer. Finally, on the off chance that I might be sending, but not receiving, I asked them to rock their wings if they heard me. They started rocking their wings almost immediately, and I felt a whole lot better right away!

As soon as the sun got over the mountain, I used my signal mirror to show them my location. (I was later warned about this by some of my rescuers, who told me that whenever they saw flashes on the ground they assumed that it was ground fire, and attacked the area of the flashes. Fortunately, I had told them I that I was using the mirror.)

About 0815 two H-34 helicopters showed up, and began searching for us. Although the A-1 pilots had my position spotted, the helicopters were having a real rough time finding us. One of them was searching the area of the hill below me, and I was frantically telling him, "I'm at your six, slightly high . . . back here!" He had just turned around, and started for me, when the enemy opened up on him with a heavy machine gun. He took a hit in his main fuel cell, and started streaming fuel. I hollered for him to clear out, and he did. The other helicopter went with him, escorting him back to his base.

Just after the helicopter was hit, and limped off to a safe area, I heard a man approaching my position. I got down on my stomach and hid in the thick undergrowth. I watched him walk to within eight feet of my position, and I was petrified! I thought for sure that he had seen me! My heart was pounding so loud that he should have been able to hear it! Either he saw me, and was afraid to take any action, or he missed me because of the thick underbrush . . . I'm still not sure which, but I'll never forget the feeling of being hunted by many men with guns, with death or capture imminent. It's a feeling that is difficult to describe . . . except to say that you're damn scared! I was glad that I had made the decision not to carry a sidearm. I think I would have been tempted to shoot him, then call on the radio for the helicopter to get me out . . . and of course, they couldn't have, and it would have been all over for me.

Now things really got tense. I knew that I should move to a more open area, to make the rescue effort easier when the helicopters returned, but I couldn't. I could hear people all around me, searching the jungle. I decided that if the helos didn't come back, or if they couldn't get me that day, that I would wait and move again that night.

I think the longest three hours of my life were that morning, while I awaited the return of the helicopters. Two of our A-6's had arrived on station, and I tried calling them. They heard me, but of course I couldn't know this since I had no receiver. Don Eaton had a receiver, but no transmitter, so he could hear what was going on, but couldn't tell anyone where he was. Fortunately, he was in a more open area, and the enemy was concentrating their search efforts in my area. The A-1's were joined by some Laotian T-28's and USAF F-105's, and they remained on station all morning, relieving each other periodically to return to base for fuel. I became convinced that morning of the effectiveness of the A-1 in the rescue role. Many other aircrewmen also found out how good the A-1 was.

About 1130 the helicopters returned. I was able to transmit to them, and as soon as the A-1's and T-28's heard their acknowledgements, the planes began to attack a little village about 80 to 100 yards from my position. (I hadn't realized that I was so close to the enemy.) They started a large fire with their 20mm and rockets . . . lots of secondary explosions, so evidently the enemy had plenty of ammo stored in the village. The fire was really going strong, and it had me a little worried, because the jungle was pretty dry in that area. Luckily, the wind was blowing the fire away from me, and it never caused a problem. While the A-1's and Thuds were strafing and bombing, the helicopters were searching for Don and I.

Don had done a lot of moving that morning, in spite of his many hurts. At the time he thought they wouldn't get to him, since he didn't have a transmitter. As soon as he heard the helicopters return, he ran to the top of a small hill and lit a smoke flare. They didn't spot the first one, so he lit another and waved it over his head. One of the T-28's spotted it and dove for him. It suddenly occurred to him that the T-28 pilot might have mistaken him for an enemy soldier, and he hit the deck. But the T-28 pulled out over him, dropped a wing, and as Don looked up, the pilot waved at him. Don waved back, and the T-28 rocked its wings. Shortly after that, one of the helicopters landed nearby and picked Don up.

In the meantime, I was calling the helicopters, trying to give them my position. I was in deep undergrowth, and I was sure that they were going to have a tough time spotting me, so I decided on what I considered to be a last ditch maneuver. I called them and told them that the next time they came over me, I would light a smoke flare. Shortly after that, one of them came over, and I lit the flare. One of the crewmen spotted me right away and waved . . . but the chopper kept right on going! I couldn't imagine at the time what had gone wrong. I later learned that the crewman who saw me didn't have a headset . . . he was a Thai door gunner, who couldn't speak English well enough to make the pilot understand that he had spotted me. Now the A-1's were really plastering the village, and I was getting increasingly nervous about it. I decided to move to a more open area regardless of the danger. I began running . . . really crashing, I guess would be more accurate, . . . through the jungle. I got to an area that had a big tall canopy tree, which was an ideal landmark. I called the helicopter and told him that I was directly up hill from the big canopy tree, and he came over my position almost immediately.

They hovered over me and started reeling out the cable with a horse collar on the end. The rotor downwash was terrific . . . bending all the brush over, and blowing the sling around. The sling kept getting caught in the trees, and it seemed like an hour until they got all the cable out. When they finally did get it all out, it was about three feet above me, and downhill . . . they couldn't get it any closer because of the tree. I was going to have to jump for it. I dropped all my survival gear and made a desperation leap for the sling. I just managed to get one arm through it, and found myself being dragged through the edge of the tree and out over the valley. It took them about three minutes to hoist me aboard. I was hanging in the horse collar by one arm, grasping my wrist with the other hand, while the helo was flying approximately 60 knots and climbing for altitude. The troops on the ground were shooting at me, and the A-1's were diving below me, firing at the enemy. I was at least 2,000 feet in the air over the valley floor before they finally pulled me into the helicopter. The first person I saw as they pulled me in was Don Eaton. He was huddled in the rear of the helicopter. What a welcome sight! We were like a couple of kids on Christmas, congratulating each other on our good fortune. They took us back to a safe area, and we caught an Air America flight for Udorn, where we were debriefed. After debriefing, we tried to go on liberty in Udorn, but we were too tired and worn out after our ordeal.

The following day we were flown back aboard the USS Independence by an E-1B, the COD. Captain Duke Windsor, the skipper of Independence, had planned a reception for us, complete with brass band and cheering shipmates. We were the first in the air wing to go down, and everyone was elated that we had been rescued. On the day after our return to the ship, they flew us to Cubi Point in the COD so that we could call our wives. The wives had been messaged when we went down, and again when we were rescued, but we wanted to reassure them that we were in good shape.

The day after our return from Cubi Point was an important one on the USS Independence. I was squadron duty officer, and was not flying, so I had a chance to observe most of the visit of the Secretary of Defense, Robert MacNamara. Mr. MacNamara attended the briefing for the big alpha strike that had been planned for that day on the Thanh Hoa power plant. Commander Jerry Denton, the air wing Operations Officer, was leading the strike and the Secretary of Defense, after attending the brief, acted as catapult officer to launch Jerry's A-6. Unfortunately, we lost Jerry Denton and his Bombadier/Navigator, Bill Tschudy, on this mission. They were the first to roll in and were hit almost immediately. They ejected and were captured. Jerry Denton landed in the center of the Thanh Hoa River. He released his parachute and attempted to swim under water to evade the enemy. However, he was captured a short time later by several enemy soldiers in a boat. Bill Tschudy landed in the middle of a courtyard, and was captured almost as soon as he touched down. We were all saddened at this loss . . . our first in combat over the north. Commander Denton had been scheduled to assume command of VA-75 the very next day. Commander "Swoose" Snead remained our Commanding Officer until word came from Washington to promote Commander Mike Vogt to the post.

On the day following this mission, I resumed flying. My first mission was to act as a tanker aircraft for the A-4's which were performing RESCAP duties in the futile attempt at recovering Denton and Tschudy. I was up for three hours and refueled several of the A-4's. They gave it a good try, but the North Vietnamese had long since captured Denton and Tschudy.

We lost our third A-6 six days later. LCDR Deke Bordone and his B/N LtJG Pete Moffet were hit at low altitude. The airplane started a slow, uncontrollable, roll and they were forced to eject in a nearly inverted position. Both were severely injured. Fortunately, they were only down about 4 hours before the helicopters got into the area and rescued them. Pete Moffet was so severely injured that he never again flew an ejection seat airplane. Deke was more fortunate. After a period of convalescence, he returned for another cruise, this time with VA-85, and flew many combat missions. He was eventually promoted to commanding officer of VA-75, and later served as CAG-3 on the USS Saratoga, leading strikes against the north during the heavy bombing just prior to the end of the war.

We had lost three airplanes and two crews in twelve days on the line, and the Navy was alarmed. They conducted an investigation, the upshot of which was to stop daylight VFR bombing in the A-6. It was just too expensive (about six million dollars per copy at that time) to allow it to be used for high risk, low value targets. The only exception to this rule was when the A-6's were used to lead the ALPHA Strikes in. (Strikes in which the entire air group was committed as a unit.) Our three lost airplanes were replaced with brand new A-6's, which were flown across the Pacific. The crews were not replaced, and as a result, the rest of us began to get a lot more flying time. We had started with 14 crews and 12 airplanes. Now we were down to 12 and 12, so we began flying double flight cycles. The flights now lasted three hours instead of the customary hour and a half. The normal flight then would consist of a two plane section taking off for strikes on pre-planned targets, with targets of opportunity as back-ups. The missions would last three hours, two of which were over North Vietnam. We liked to have two planes on these missions, because if one got in trouble, he knew the other was in the vicinity and could radio for help or spot the position of the downed airplane. We got a lot of night flying on these missions.

After about 30 days on Yankee Station, we pulled back to Cubi Point for some rest and relaxation. I always enjoyed Cubi because of the fine golf course they had, and the excellent Officers Club on the hill. The little town of Olongapo, which was adjacent to Cubi, turned into quite a prosperous city. Thousands of Fillipinos had migrated to it, just to get the dollars from the sailors and marines on liberty. And the money was really spent after those long at-sea periods!

After Cubi, we were back on Yankee Station for another 35 day line period. Fortunately, VA-75 did not lose any people during this period, but the air wing did lose an A-4 pilot and an F-4 crew.

Our next liberty period was in Cubi, and several of us traveled to Manila. Then the ship sailed to Hong Kong. I was able to play a lot of golf, and really enjoyed myself. On one of our rounds at the Royal Hong Kong Golf Club, CDR Mike Vogt, the skipper, had a hole-in-one. I watched the ball roll into the cup from 160 yards out, and I said, "You just made a hole-in-one, Skipper!" The officers and men really enjoyed liberty and shopping in Hong Kong and we hated to leave that fascinating city.

Back on the line again, we resumed our night bombing of North Vietnam. On our very first night back, I had two flights, totaling about 6 hours of flight time. I was plenty tired after that one! The reason I had two flights was that I had been scheduled as "go" bird on the first mission that night, which I flew. Upon my return, I was briefed as standby for the next mission. I had no real expectation of going, but when the number two A-6 went "down" on the deck, I was taxied forward, launched, and flew the mission. I'll bet I developed 25 gray hairs and lost two years off of my life on that night.

The most terrifying night of my life, in an airplane, occurred the night I flew a mission with Lt. Doug Bibler. This was my first night flight after being rescued, and Don Eaton was still not medically fit for flying. The two hours we spent over North Vietnam were relatively uneventful . . . I think we bombed a truck park, or something. But I'll never forget the return to the ship. It was a classic example of how Navy Pilots earn the right to sleep and eat in air conditioned comfort aboard ship.

Ordinarily, a night landing aboard the carrier is not too scary. But on this occasion, the ship was steaming through a thunderstorm. It was the only cloud within twenty miles, and the ship was right under the middle of it. I proceeded inbound and at ten miles from the ship, I was hit with a terrific case of vertigo. I would have bet a million dollars that I was flying 90 degrees right wing down! I knew better, of course, from looking at my instruments, which indicated that I was flying straight and level. However, it would have been very easy to ignore them and fly by the seat of my pants. I told Doug that I had vertigo, and asked him to monitor the attitude instruments to make sure that I didn't succumb to the vertigo. I approached the ship for my landing, and at three miles I started my let-down under Carrier Controlled Approach. At three quarters of a mile I was told to take over visually and call "meat ball". (At that point I should have been able to see the meatball of the fresnel landing system aboard the ship.) I looked out the windscreen and couldn't see a thing! I decided to take my own wave-off, and added power. Suddenly, the island structure of the carrier loomed up! We flew right by it, narrowly missing a collision! I flew upwind into the bolter pattern, the vertigo still raging in me. I told Doug that I would try one more pass, and if we didn't make it aboard, I was going to divert on my own to Danang. Normally this isn't up to the individual pilot . . . the Captain of the ship makes the decision whether or not the plane is to continue in the pattern. But my vertigo was so bad that I felt that we wouldn't live through more than one more pass. I got my instructions from CCA to turn downwind, and when we were directly abeam of the ship, I looked out the left side of the canopy and spotted it. We continued on our approach. I turned on the windscreen air full blast, and this seemed to help to clear some of the heavy rain from the windscreen, because I could just barely make out the ship. I still couldn't pick up the meatball, and the LSO talked me into a complete landing. I don't remember if we caught the three or four wire, but we did get aboard. We taxied up on the bow, shut down the airplane, opened the canopy and got out. I climbed down and literally kissed the flight deck! It was raining as hard as I had seen it rain anywhere! I went down to the ready room still shaking . . . that was the worst experience I had ever had aboard a carrier, and I attribute our safe landing to Lt. Doug

Bibler's outstanding crew concept, calmness, and professionalism during the approach.

Along about the middle of September, one of our airplanes was due for a maintenance cycle, and Don Eaton and I were picked to ferry it to Cubi, where the squadron had a maintenance team standing by. We manned the aircraft, taxied to the catapult, and added 100% power. The cat officer touched the deck and we were catapulted into the air. I reached up to raise the gear as soon as we were airborne, and the A-6 was racked by a tremendous explosion! I went right to the instruments, but couldn't see any sign of trouble. In the meantime, the gear had come up and we started to lose altitude. Fortunately, the flaps were still down and their added lift kept us airborne. It was about five o'clock in the afternoon, and the sun was directly over my shoulder, shining onto the instrument panel . . . so I didn't see that the starboard fire warning light was on! I looked back at the instruments, and spotted the light. I immediately told Don Eaton that I had a light, and that I was shutting down the starboard engine. (I did this because in times of panic pilots have been known to shut down the wrong engine, and I wanted him to verify that I was shutting down the proper engine.) I shut down the engine and continued to climb until I had enough airspeed to raise the flaps. We tried to contact the ship on the radio, but for some reason the radio decided to quit working right then. We couldn't contact anyone. I flew back over the ship, not knowing if I was on fire, or what my problem might be. I spotted an A-3 tanker that had been orbiting, prior to landing and decided to join on him in the hope that I could communicate with him through hand signals. (Our receivers were working, so we could hear what was said on the radio, but we still couldn't talk to anyone.) I joined on the A-3 and began giving him all kinds of hand signals . . . asking him to look me over . . . did I have a fire? In the engine? . . . and many others . . . none of which he seemed capable of understanding. He radioed the ship that he had an A-6 on his wing that wanted to land immediately. I shook my head vigorously no . . I was too heavy . . couldn't land. (I had lost my fuel dump capability too.) We continued to orbit, still unaware of what our exact problem was. Finally Don hit on the idea of getting his survival radio out and calling the A-3 on the guard channel. We managed to tell him about the fire warning light, and the secured engine. About that time, he looked back and noticed that the whole starboard rear engine cover and tailpipe had been blown off our airplane. He called the ship and advised them of our problem. At that time the A-6 had not yet had a single engine landing aboard ship and the captain decided it would be better if we diverted to Danang. We made an uneventful landing at Danang and taxied to the parking area. When I got out of the airplane and saw the mess that explosion had made of the right side of the airplane, I realized how lucky we had been to get it back safely.

We spent the night at Danang and were treated to a big beer party by the Air Force pilots there. About 0300, an F-8 pilot who had been diverted to Danang came in and told me that he had heard that a "Flying Ace" aircraft had been lost over North Vietnam. "Flying Ace" was VA-75's tactical call sign, so I was pretty worried at the thought that more of my buddies had been shot down. The primitive sleeping quarters at Danang, along with my anxiety over who had been lost, kept me from getting much sleep that night. It was hotter than blazes, two rocket raids were called, and we were sleeping in tents that seemed to hold all of the heat of the day, all through the night.

The next morning the COD came in to get us, and I learned that the Squadron Commander, Mike Vogt, and his B/N Red Barber, had been lost, and that there was virtually no hope for their survival. It was a tragic loss. Mike Vogt left a widow and five children and Red Barber was mourned by a family. In addition, Red had almost been the father of the Navy A-6 program. He had been an enlisted man and had risen through the ranks to Lieutenant. He knew the A-6 forwards and backwards, including all of its myriad avionics systems. The COD flight back to the ship was permeated with gloom. Commander Warwick, who had started the cruise as number three on the squadron seniority list, as maintenance officer, was now the CO. We were down to eleven crews. They replaced our two airplanes, and a week later we got another crew, fresh out of VA-42, the RAG.

One of the scariest missions for me personally was the daylight ALPHA Strike, in which about twenty-four aircraft struck the same target simultaneously. And the one particular mission that stands out in my mind is the one in which we got the Kep highway bridge.

Four A-6's led the strike, and this is when we saw the first SAM missiles fired. They shot thirteen SAM's at the strike aircraft, and the CO of one of the F-4 squadrons said one of them came so close to him that he could read the missile serial number on its side! Fortunately, something was faulty and it didn't detonate. I saw a couple of them myself, though they weren't that close to me. I remember rolling in on the target . . . each A-6 carried five 2,000 pound bombs, so after the first A-6 had dropped, the target was pretty well obscured by smoke and dust. We got the bridge, but there was a dike just about 200 to 300 yards down the river that the supply trucks could drive over, so it was really no big deal to the North Vietnamese . . . and we lost an F-4 and an A-4 during that mission. We flew right over Kep airfield, and we could see the Migs on the ground . . . though they didn't come up after us.

We had five or six of those air wing strikes during the last part of the cruise, and as I said, they were the scariest for me personally. I would much rather fly an A-6 by myself, at night, over North Vietnam than to go on one of those ALPHA Strikes. I think the results of those strikes were outstanding, but the losses were pretty heavy for us too. I would hate to be on the ground when one of those ALPHA Strikes came in. The North Vietnamese would fire every conceivable type of ammunition at us, in abundance, and everything that goes up must come down, so you know that the people on the ground were subjected to a rain of shrapnel, not to mention the SAMs that went ballistic and exploded when they hit the ground.

Our next in-port period was spent in Japan. We had eight days there,

Loading and checking 500lb. Snakeye bombs prior to 1968 strike from the USS Ranger. (U.S. Navy)

A-6A of VA-165, loaded with 500lb Snakeyes leaves the waist cat of the Ranger enroute to North Vietnam, January 1968. (U.S. Navy)

which was ample time in which to take in the sights and to play some golf.

We went back to Yankee Station for our last line period, which was due to end in mid-November. All of us were counting the days until we were due to head for home. This last line period was relatively uneventful, and we steamed for home right on schedule. We stopped at Cubi enroute, and off-loaded a lot of our spare A-6 parts. These were earmarked for VA-85, which was coming on line with the USS Kitty Hawk, for the second A-6 deployment.

Our big homecoming took place on December 10, 1965. We launched the entire air wing from 150 miles at sea, joined into a long trail formation, and headed for Oceana NAS. Every flyable airplane was in the air, and it was a pretty impressive formation. We overflew Oceana at 500 feet, split up, and made our landings. Of course, all of the wives and children were there to greet us, so it was a real homecoming. They had champagne for us and Miss Virginia Beach was there to give all the aircrewmen a kiss . . . though I don't think she kissed many . . . just the bachelors.

When I reflected on what I had seen during our five and a half months on Yankee Station, I decided that there was no chance of the war ending in the next five years if we continued to run it in the manner in which I had seen it run. Unfortunately, my estimate was all too correct."

Intruder of VA-85, the second A-6 squadron to enter combat during a training flight over Virginia prior to 1965 combat deployment. Rudder is yellow, with white "Falcons". (USN)

A-6A of VA-35, crewed by LTJG John Swanson and LTJG Leonard became the 200,000th aircraft to land aboard the USS Coral Sea in August, 1969. (USN)

VA-35 Intruder aboard the USS America, off the Florida coast in 1973. (Jim Brady via Jim Sullivan)

VAH-123 A-6A at Edwards FTC in 1967. Tail bands are gold, edged in black. (via Jim Sullivan)

VA-85 Intruder displays 1968 markings, red tail band over black letters. (Roger Besecker via Jim Sullivan)

VA-165 "Boomers" Intruder is made ready for launch from USS Constellation for a 1972 strike against North Vietnam during the climatic stages of the Vietnam War. (U.S. Navy)

Being directed to the cat, Intruder begins to spread its wings. USS Constellation, Tonkin Gulf, April, 1972. (USN)

Flight deck action in the Gulf of Tonkin during the spring of 1972. (USN)

Red-shirted ordnancemen strain to load a 500lb bomb aboard an A-6 of VA-85, aboard the USS America, 1968. (USN)

U.S. Air Force aircrewmen on exchange duty with Navy Attack Squadron 165 flew combat missions from the USS Constellation in 1972. At left, B/N Maj. Doyle Ballentine checks bomb load prior to strike. Above, Major Larry Beasley deplanes, post-mission. (USAF)

Canopy Development

A-6 of VA-196, configured for an anti-SAM missile site mission, with standard ARM on port pylon and Shrike on starboard pylon, seconds before launch from Constellation in 1968. (USN)

VA-196 Intruder returns to USS Enterprise with its full complement of Standard ARMs and Shrikes after a 1972 mission. (Bruce Smith)

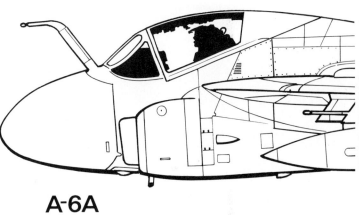

A-6A

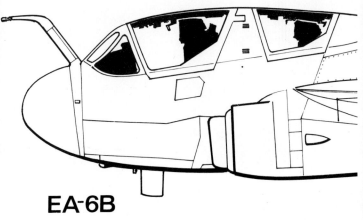

EA-6B

A-6A of VA-35, loaded with 5 3,000lb bombs trails condensation from wingtips as it begins its roll-in on bridge busting mission. (USN)

VA-165 Intruder overflies Shaw AFB, S.C. in 1970 (Jim Sullivan)

VA-165 Intruder leaves the waist cat of the Ranger enroute to strike on North Vietnam. (USN)

Intruder of VA-145 catches the number four wire on return to Ranger. (Jan Jacobs via Sullivan)

VA-52 "Knight Riders" A-6, sporting blue knights helmet on vertical fin displays empty TERs at NAS LeMoore in 1969. This is the aircraft of squadron commanded CDR Jim McKenzie. (Duane Kasulka via Norman Taylor)

A-6E of VA-75 "Sunday Punchers". This aircraft flown by CAG . . . the Air Wing Commander.

A-6A of VA-115 being hauled to a stop aboard the USS Midway.
Leading edge slats are out, but wingtip speed brakes
are beginning to close.

KA-6D of VA-176. The tanker version of the A-6 does not retain weapons delivery capability, the avionics of the rear extensible platform having been removed. The all-weather cockpit displays are likewise removed. It is capable of carrying 3,844 gallons of fuel, 3,000 of which are transferrable. (Charles Howes)

A-6A of VMA(AW)-224 at MCAS Cherry Point, N.C., 7/74. (Jim Sullivan)

EA-6B of VAQ-133. This aircraft was flown by CDR Jim Wheeler, VAQ-133 Executive Officer.

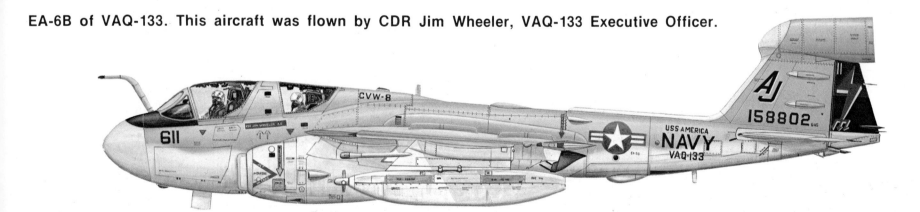

. . . and heads back to Danang. First Marine deployment of the Intruder to Vietnam was made by VMA(AW)-242 in November, 1966. They were supported by VMCJ-2's EA-6A's.

VMA(AW)-533 Intruder unloads 8,000lbs. of bombs on a "skyspot" radar controlled bombing mission in support of the 7th Marines west of Danang, December, 1967. (USMC)

Marine Intruder catches the SATS arresting gear upon return to Chu Lai. Marine Intruders were operated under some of the most primitive conditions imaginable, which caused constant headaches for avionics maintenance personnel. (USMC)

VMA(AW)-242 was first Marine Intruder squadron to deploy to Vietnam. A majority of its missions were night interdiction raids deep into North Vietnam, though many times they were called upon to provide pinpoint close support for beleaguered Marine ground forces. (USMC)

Intruder of 242 "Batmen" enroute to target. Close proximity of battlefields to Intruder airfields allowed operations sans wing fuel tanks on close support missions. (USMC)

VMA(AW)-225 A-6 demonstrates SATS catapult capabilities at Bogue Field, Camp Lejeune, N.C., 1968. (USMC)

A-6B of VMA(AW)-242 at Kelly AFB, Texas in February, 1973. Black rudder with white shield and black "bat", gold lightning flash. "B" model is externally identical to the "A". It was originally intended as an avionics stripped VFR attacker, but later was configured to deliver Standard ARM anti-radiation missiles. (Norman E. Taylor)

VMCJ-1 EA-6A at Danang in 1970. EA-6A's replaced the EF-10B Skyknight in Marine's aerial inventory. They provide tactical ECM for the Marine's strike aircraft. (USMC)

EA-6A tail displays the colorful marking of VMCJ-1 at MCAS Iwakuni, Japan. Dark blue circle outline, red "one", gold eagle and lightning flash. (H. Nagakubo via Norman Taylor)

29

EA-6A, carrying external fuel tanks and jamming pods, flies by NAF Atsugi, October, 1973. It was home-based at MCAS Iwakuni, Japan. (S. Ohtaki via Norman E. Taylor)

A-6A (later converted to A-6C) of VMA(AW)-533, based at MCAS Iwakuni, Japan in 1973. Markings for this aircraft contained on Micro-Scale decal sheet number 72-79. Photo at left shows outboard pylon mounted AN/ALQ-100 forward ECM antenna to good advantage. Rear antennas are mounted on vertical fin and rudder. (H. Nagakubo via Norman E. Taylor)

A-6C, BuNo 155692, illustrated on preceding page. Principle change incorporated in "C" model is its ability to deploy TRIM. (Trails, Roads, Interdiction, Multisensor.) TRIM is turret mounted forward-looking infrared and low light level television system. (H. Nagakubo via Norman E. Taylor)

EA-6A of VMCJ-1. MCAS Iwakuni, Japan, 1973. (H. Nagakubo via Norman Taylor)

EA-6A of VMCJ-2 at MCAS Cherry Point in 1973. (Jim Sullivan)

Rear view of A-6A shows fin-mounted ECM antenna. (Jim Sullivan)

A-6B of VMA(AW)-224, MCAS Cherry Point, N.C., displays wing tank graffiti which it acquired compliments of VMA(AW)-242 ground crew. (Jim Sullivan)

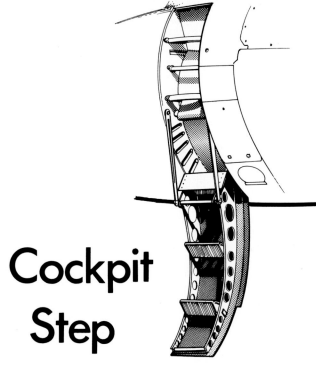

Cockpit Step

A-6B of VMA(AW)-121 about to touch down at MCAS Cherry Point, N.C., 1973. Wingtip speed brakes are in full-open position. (Jim Sullivan)

A-6E of VMA(AW)-121. All white vertical fin is adorned with dark green horsehead with gold collar, eyes, black trim. (Dr. J.G. Handelman)

Intruder of VMA(AW)-332 BuNo 154167, MCAS Cherry Point, 1971. White rudder and drop tanks carry red polka dots. (Jim Sullivan)

Intruders of VMA(AW)-224 display markings applied for their deployment aboard USS Coral Sea in 1972. Marine A-6 squadrons periodically operate from Navy carriers. (Jim Sullivan)

A-6 of VMAT(AW)-202 at MCAS Cherry Point, 1972. (Jim Sullivan)

EA-6B ECM Pod

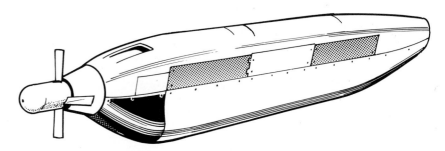

Polkadots Intruder. Red leading edge on rudder, yellow hat and cane. Note that lift spoiler on top of starboard wing is slightly open. (Jim Sullivan)

ALQ-99 High-Power Noise Jamming System

A-6's of VA-176 approach USS Franklin D. Roosevelt in the Caribbean after a simulated Alpha Strike in 1969. (USN)

VA-34 A-6 about to trap aboard the British Carrier Ark Royal. A-6 was the first nose tow aircraft to be catapulted from a British carrier. (USN)

A-6A of VA-85 leaves the waist cat of the USS Kitty Hawk during South China Sea operations in 1965. (Lionel Paul via Jim Sullivan)

VA-85 Intruder about to catch the number two wire aboard CVA-63 in the Tonkin Gulf, 1965. (via Jim Sullivan)

Landing Gear

Nose

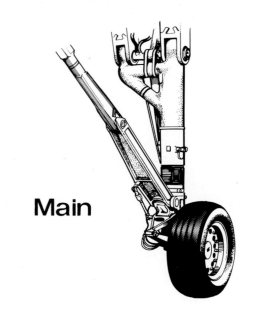

Main

36

VA-176 A-6A over the Caribbean. Excellent visibility afforded by the A-6 cockpit is evident. (USN)

VA-176 A-6A's, circa 1969. (USN)

One of life's little dramas. VMAT(AW)-202 A-6 encountered difficulty in getting left main gear to extend for landing at MCAS Cherry Point, 1971. He flew by tower for visual confirmation of his problem, (above) took it back to altitude, "shook" the recalcitrant gear down, then declared an emergency and requested an arrested landing. He had two "bolters" on field arrestment gear before finally catching the wire in an anti-climactic landing. (Jim Sullivan)

VA-65 Intruder being towed aft aboard USS Kitty Hawk off the coast of California, November, 1968. (Lou Drendel)

. . . and being pulled to a halt during air operations in preparation for 1969 Combat Cruise. (Lou Drendel)

Absence of launch and hold-back cables makes evident the advantages of the nosetow link launching mechanism, which the Intruder introduced to the fleet. (Lou Drendel)

A-6 pilot and B/N head for their VA-165 Intruder prior to 1972 strike on North Vietnamese targets. International orange flight suits and white helmet were taboo for most aircrews during the war. (USN)

A-6B of VA-115 "Arabs" carrying 300 gallon drop tanks and empty MER's. See Color profile for markings details. (S. Ohtaki via Norman E. Taylor)

A-6 of VA-115 carries rainbow colors on top of vertical fin. It was flown by Cdr. Lew Chatham, CAG, CAW 5. At Misawa AB, Japan, Sept. 1974. (Norman E. Taylor)

A-6 of VA-52. NAS North Island, August, 1973. (Robert Lawson via Jim Sullivan)

A-6 of VA-115 off the USS Midway. (Norman E. Taylor)

A-6A of VA-176, NAS Oceana, Va. April, 1974. Red lightning bolt, white glove and "AE" outlined in red. (Jim Sullivan)

A-6E

A-6E's of VA-34 at NAS Oceana, VA, April, 1974. (Jim Sullivan)

If beauty is only skin deep,* then it may be said of the various Intruder models that effectiveness is also only skin deep. The A-6A, designed around 1950's state of the art avionics, proved the validity of the design concept, but it's first-generation electronics were fraught with maintenance problems. The A-6E is a true second generation attack aircraft. The fact that it is outwardly identical to the A-6A speaks highly for the integrity of the original airframe design. (Many A-6A's have been retrofitted with the new systems to bring them up to "E" standards.) Paramount among the advantages enjoyed by the "E" over the "A" are; Improved systems reliability, electronic maintainability improvements, and added self sustaining systems. The new systems require 35% less time by electronics technicians to keep them "on line". State of the art improvements are not limited to the above though, and the combat capabilities of the A-6E are also measurably greater than it's forerunners. The A-6E's high quality radar mapping presentation allows positive identification of both significant and non-significant radar targets. Normal radar glint has been eliminated, which allows the reproduction of cultural features in near photographic clarity. The electronics system has been mechanized using the radar and computer equipment for three axis space positioning and high accuracy aircraft-to-target velocity. The weapons release system is now solid-state, adding to it's reliability. The A-6E is powered by the J-52-P-8 engine, which develops 9,300 lbs. of thrust. It is the latest version of the time-proven J-52, and gives the A-6E an added measure of speed and maneuverability.

*Aircraft design ascetics would probably deny that the A-6 and beauty had anything at all in common.

A-6E's of VA-34 at NAS Oceana, VA, April, 1974. (Jim Sullivan)

A pair of A-6's of VA-95 "Skyknights", off the USS Coral Sea. Photo at left illustrates markings circa 1973. Photo at right illustrates 1974 markings. "00" is CAG airplane. Colors on rudder of this plane are; top to bottom, yellow, black, orange, red. Fin cap and "dragon" motif are black on both airplanes, as are "dragon's teeth" on rudder of "01". (Bruce Trombecky and Bob LaBouy via Trombecky)

CAG A-6 of VA-145. Colors on sword: red, yellow, blue, orange, green, black, maroon. Yellow lightning bolts, green fin cap. February, 1974. (G.R. Markgraf via Trombecky)

VA-145 markings carried in 1971 were black. (Bob LaBouy via Trombecky)

VA-65 "Tigers" CAG airplane, circa 1974. Markings are vivid red-orange, outlined in black. (Jim Sullivan)

KA-6D of VA-75 "Sunday Punchers". NAS Oceana, April, 1974. Note high nose number carried by KA-6's. (Jim Sullivan)

A-6's of VA-75 and VA-52 illustrate the Extensible Equipment Platform in the open position. Bulge on bottom of platform is doppler radar antenna. Equipment carried on platform includes; MA-1 compass amplifier, AN/APR-27 radar receiver, and control panel. (also golf clubs, suitcases, etc. on cross-country trips.) (Charles Howes)

VA-128 Intruder at Mather AFB, Calif., October, 1972. Markings are deep gold, outlined in black. VA-128 is based at NAS Whidbey Island. (David Menard via Norman E. Taylor)

Current markings of VA-42 "Green Pawns", the Intruder training squadron. It is illustrated with 300 gallon centerline tank. A-6 is capable of carrying almost 18,000 lbs. of fuel. (Jim Sullivan)

KA-6D of VA-85. Dark green fuselage and tail bands. (Bruce Trombecky)

Bomb-laden VA-85 Intruder off the coast of Virginia. (USN)

VA-52 Intruder. Note additional antenna on radome and under intake warning "vee". (Charles Howes)

The number three and four A-6's were still performing flight test duties at the Grumman plant on Long Island as of 1973. The no. 4 airplane was never converted to the larger of rudder of the production version. (Lionel Paul via Jim Sullivan)

A-6A of NATC's Weapons System Test branch. Lettering on centerline store reads; "Instrumentation Pod Handle with care." (Dr. J.G. Handelman)

EA-6B "Prowler" prototype flew for the first time in May, 1968. The Prowler is four seat growth version of the Marines' EA-6A. It is used by the Navy in the Tactical ECM role exclusively. It carries 8,000 lbs. of avionics internally. (USN)

Crews of test EA-6B's confer after successful test flight from NAS Patuxent River, Md. (USN)

EA-6B at Grumman's Long Island plant. Addition of second cockpit required 40" extension of fuselage. (Lionel Paul via Jim Sullivan)

EA-6B of NATC, NAS Patuxent River, Md. Test markings are black stripes, day-glo orange tail and wing sections. (Jim Sullivan)

45

Prowler of VAQ-131 (above) marking colors: medium blue stripes and lightning bolt, red and yellow helmet. VAQ-129 EA-6B (left) carries five ECM jamming pods, each weighing 950 lbs. Prowler can perform role of stand-off jammer, ECM escort for penetration protection. Pods have self-contained turbine-driven power source. Crew consists of pilot and three NFO's, who handle tactical jamming equipment. Late production Prowlers have the uprated J52-P-408 engines. (S. Ohtaki via Norman Taylor & USN)

VAQ-129 Prowler. Red lightning bolt, black outlined sword. Seven Tactical Electronic Warfare squadrons operate the EA-6B. (Bob Lawson via Sullivan)

EA-6B at NAS Lemoore, Ca., 1972. "B" can maneuver at up to 5.5 G's and has max speed of 510 knots at sea level. Gross weight of 51,000 lbs. required strengthening of airframe. (Peter Mancus via Jim Sullivan)

VAQ-132 "Scorpions" Prowler at NAS North Island, CA., August, 1973. Additional ram air scoops were required on EA-6B's at mid-fuselage because of the added electronics. (Robert Lawson via Jim Sullivan)

VAQ-134 Prowler. Black Rudder, yellow lightning bolt, maroon bird. Ejection seat backs are orange on this particular aircraft. Nose gear door is maroon. Prowlers of VAQ-132 (see photo at left) were the first to deploy in combat, aboard USS Enterprise in 1972. (Paul Stevens)

47

A-6E TRAM (Target Recognition Attack Multisensor) This configuration consists of the addition of a turreted electro-optical sensor package, containing both infrared and laser equipment. The sensor package and turret provide lower hemispheric coverage for laser-guided weapon delivery. First flight was March 22, 1974. Besides noticeable bulge under nose, note enlarged ram air scoop forward of tail. (Grumman)

Versatile Intruder acts as aerial tanker for the latest Grumman cat, the F-14A. (USN)

NEA-6A was moved from NAS China Lake to NAS Lakehurst, N.J. for FAA fuel tank rupture tests. (Roger Besecker via Norman E. Taylor)

Author's Note

I have particularly enjoyed putting this book together because it has given me the chance to tell a dual success story. As the first true all weather strike airplane, the Intruder is an unqualified success. The naval aviator whose stories provide the "in action" portions of the book has had an equally successful career.

Don Boecker and I grew up together, sharing the experiences of grammar and high school. Upon graduation from Naperville Community High School, Don attended Columbian Prep for a year, then went on to the U.S. Naval Academy at Annapolis. He graduated from Annapolis in 1960, and the following fall reported to Pensacola to commence flight training. He was designated a Naval Aviator in 1962 and reported to VA-43 for training in the A-4C. He then served with VA-76 aboard the USS Enterprise, making two Mediterranean deployments and participating in the Cuban Blockade during the Missile Crisis.

In September, 1963 he transferred to VA-75. His experiences in VA-75 are related elsewhere in this book.

In September 1966, Don reported to NAS Patuxent River, Md., where he attended the U.S. Naval Test Pilot School. He graduated in June, 1967 and was assigned to the attack branch of the Weapons System Test Division where he served as project pilot for the Navy Preliminary Evaluation and later on the Board of Inspection Survey Trials for the TC-4C. He also flew project flights to evaluate new systems in A-1, A-3, A-4, A-6, A-7 and F-8 aircraft. Perhaps the crowning achievement of his tour at NATC was his assignment as team leader for a joint Navy/Air Force preliminary evaluation of the A-7D/E Corsair II at LTV in Dallas, Texas. He flew the first military flight in the A-7E, completed the joint service evaluation and later became Project Officer in charge of the Board of Inspection Survey Trials for the A-7E at NAS Patuxent River, Md. (He was a Lieutenant at the time.)

In October, 1969 he reported to VA-42 for a stint as A-6 Instructor Pilot, Squadron Personnel Officer, and later as Training Officer. He served as Maintenance Officer and Operations Officer in VA-75 during a 1970 Mediterranean deployment aboard USS Forrestal.

In April 1972, he was assigned as Plans and Programs Officer on Commander Medium Attack Wing ONE Staff at NAS Oceana. In May of 1973 he reported to VA-85 aboard the USS Forrestal, where he assumed the position of Executive Officer. On July 1, 1974, Don assumed command of VA-85.

His career has been closely linked to Naval Attack Aviation in general, and to the A-6 in particular. His one paragraph description of the A-6's capabilities provides a fitting close to "The A-6 Intruder in Action".

The A-6 has been the only true all-weather attack aircraft in the Navy inventory. As such, it was the workhorse of attack Naval Aviation during the Viet Nam conflict. Capable of close air support, interdiction, and deep strike missions, the high maneuverability with a respectable load of ordnance, best carrier safety record, internally carried ECM for protection, and . . . most importantly . . . The Crew Concept performed by two professionals all combine to make this sophisticated attack weapons system the best in the free world. With the increased weapons delivery accuracy of the latest model A-6E and the new developments now being evaluated, this airplane will continue to be a potent weapons system, capable of unleashing tremendous fire power, when tasked, well into the 1980's.

The author (right) with Don Boecker after 1969 flight in the A-6. (Author)